SCHOLASTIC

Comprehension Skills

40 Short Passages for Close Reading

GRADE 4

Linda Ward Beech

Rohan

New York • Toronto • London • Auckland • Sydney
Mexico City • New Delhi • Hong Kong • Buenos Aires

Teaching
Resources

The reading passages in this book were selected and adapted from the following titles in the series,
35 Reading Passages for Comprehension: *Context Clues & Figurative Language, Inferences & Drawing Conclusions, Main Ideas & Summarizing,* and *Point of View & Fact and Opinion* (Scholastic, 2006).
Copyright © 2006 by Linda Ward Beech.

Cover design by Jorge J. Namerow
Interior design by Jason Robinson
Illustrations by Mike Gordon

ISBN: 978-0-545-46055-2
Text copyright © 2012 by Linda Ward Beech
Illustrations copyright © 2012 by Scholastic Inc.
Published by Scholastic Inc.
All rights reserved.
Printed in the U.S.A.

21   40   24 23 22

Contents

Passages

Comprehension Skills: 40 Short Passages for Close Reading, Grade 4 • © 2012 by Linda Ward Beech, Scholastic Teaching Resources

Using This Book

Reading comprehension in nonfiction involves numerous thinking skills. Students require these skills to make sense of a text and become successful readers. This book offers practice in key skills needed to meet the Common Core State Standards in Reading/Language Arts for grade four. (See page 6 for more.) Each student page includes a short passage focusing on four of these essential comprehension skills.

Comprehension Skills At-a-Glance

Use the information that follows to introduce the reading comprehension skills covered in this book.

Main Idea & Details

Understanding the main or key idea of a paragraph is crucial for a reader. The main idea is what the paragraph is about. The other parts of the paragraph help to explain more about this key idea. The main idea is sometimes in the first or last sentence of a paragraph. Students should be aware that some main ideas are stated explicitly and others are implicit requiring readers to put together details to determine the main idea.

The information that supports the main idea is usually referred to as the details. Details—facts, examples, definitions, etc.—help a reader gain a fuller understanding of a paragraph.

Summarize

Readers should be able to use main ideas to summarize a text. By summarizing, students are better able to recall important points. This is an important skill for taking notes and studying for exams.

Context Clues

Using context clues means determining an unfamiliar word's meaning by studying the phrases, sentences, and overall text with which the word appears. Context clues help readers comprehend and enjoy a text and also read more smoothly and efficiently.

In this paragraph, students have to read the entire text and ask themselves "What is this paragraph mainly about?" The main idea is supported by different facts (details) about the story of the "Happy Birthday" song.

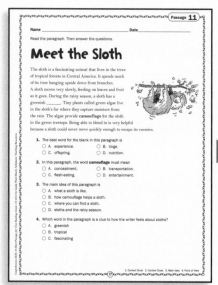

Several clues in the paragraph (*greenish tinge*, *green treetops*, *blend in*) help a reader determine the meaning of *camouflage*.

4

Figurative Language

Beyond using context clues to derive meaning is the ability to differentiate between literal and figurative language. Readers who can recognize figures of speech and determine their meanings are well on their way to fluency.

Inference

Although some students don't know what an inference is, many are most likely making inferences—both in their daily lives and when reading—without being aware of it. Students should understand that writers don't include every detail in their work; it is up to readers to supply some information. A reader makes a guess or inference by putting together what is in a text with what he or she already knows. Inferring makes a significant difference in how much a reader gains from a text.

Draw Conclusions

After thinking about information in a text, a reader makes a decision or conclusion by examining evidence rooted in the text. Students should know that writers don't always state all of their ideas, so readers have to look for clues to understand what is meant.

Fact & Opinion

Readers who can identify and differentiate between statements of fact and opinion are better able to analyze and assess a text. Students should learn to recognize phrases, such as *I think*, *you should*, and *it's the best/most*, that signal opinions.

Point of View

While distinguishing fact from opinion is one step in the reading process, it is important for students to go further. They should be able to sort facts, opinions, and feelings to help determine a writer's point of view and compare it to what they themselves think. Students should learn that good readers consult several sources on subjects of interest to gain different points of view.

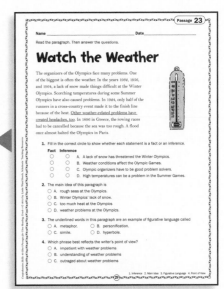

The writer never says that Olympic organizers have to be good problem solvers, but facts in the paragraph plus what readers know about organizing events can be used to make an inference.

To appreciate this text, the reader should understand that the writer has inserted commentary or opinion into the paragraph. For example, the sentence, *Maybe they don't know which words to capitalize!*, is the author's opinion

Tips

★ Tell students to first read the passage and then answer the questions. Show them how to fill in the circles for bubble-test questions.

★ The comprehension skills targeted in the questions accompanying each passage are labeled at the bottom of the page.

★ Review the completed pages with students on a regular basis. Encourage them to explain their thinking for each correct answer.

Comprehension Skills: 40 Short Passages for Close Reading, Grade 4 © 2012 by Linda Ward Beech, Scholastic Teaching Resources

Meeting the Common Core State Standards

The passages and comprehension questions in this book are designed to help you meet both your specific English/Language Arts standards and learning expectations as well as those recommended by the Common Core State Standards Initiative (CCSSI). The activities in this book align with the following CCSSI standards for grade four.

Reading Standards for Informational Text

Key Ideas and Details

1. Refer to details and examples in a text when explaining what the text says explicitly and when drawing inferences from the text.
2. Determine the main idea of a text and explain how it is supported by key details; summarize the text.
3. Explain events, procedures, ideas, or concepts in a historical, scientific, or technical text, including what happened and why, based on specific information in the text.

Craft and Structure

4. Determine the meaning of general academic and domain-specific words and phrases in a text relevant to a *grade 4 topic or subject area*.
5. Describe the overall structure (e.g., chronology, comparison, cause/effect, problem/solution) of events, ideas, concepts, or information in a text or part of a text.

Integration of Knowledge and Ideas

8. Explain how an author uses reasons and evidence to support particular points in a text.

Range of Reading and Level of Text Complexity

10. By the end of year, read and comprehend informational texts, including history/social studies, science, and technical texts, in the grades 4–5 text complexity band proficiently, with scaffolding as needed at the high end of the range.

Reading Standards: Foundational Skills

Fluency

4. Read with sufficient accuracy and fluency to support comprehension.
   a. Read on-level text with purpose and understanding.
   c. Use context to confirm or self-correct word recognition and understanding, rereading as necessary.

Language Standards

Knowledge of Language

3. Use knowledge of language and its conventions when writing, speaking, reading, or listening.

Vocabulary Acquisition and Use

4. Determine or clarify the meaning of unknown and multiple-meaning words and phrases based on *grade 4 reading and content*, choosing flexibly from a range of strategies.
   a. Use context (e.g., cause/effect relationships and comparisons in text) as a clue to the meaning of a word or phrase.
5. Demonstrate understanding of figurative language, word relationships, and nuances in word meanings.
   a. Explain the meaning of simple similes and metaphors in context.
6. Acquire and use accurately grade-appropriate general academic and domain-specific words and phrases, including those that signal precise actions, emotions, or states of being and that are basic to a particular topic.

Comprehension Skills: 40 Short Passages for Close Reading, Grade 4 © 2012 by Linda Ward Beech, Scholastic Teaching Resources

Name Rohan   **Date** 6/5/23

Read the paragraph. Then answer the questions.

About Hippos

The hippopotamus spends a lot of time in water. In fact, the name of this amazing African animal means "river horse." During a hot day, a hippo will spend hours in rivers and lakes. Only its eyes, ears, and nostrils can be seen above the water. This helps to keep the hairless animal from getting sunburned. Although it eats water plants, the hippo goes ashore at night to find larger plants. If it is the dry season and the water is low, a hippo rolls in mud to cover its huge body. This way its skin doesn't dry out

1. The main idea of this paragraph is
   ○ A. a hippopotamus is a water horse.
   ○ B. this animal is a plant-eater.
   ○ C. hippos live only in Africa.
   ◉ D. a hippo spends a lot of time in water.

2. A supporting detail is
   ○ A. sometimes hippos overturn boats.
   ○ B. sunburn is a problem for many animals.
   ○ C. a hippo likes to roll in mud.
   ◉ D. water protects a hippo's skin from the sun.

3. Which word in the passage is a clue to how the writer feels about hippos?
   ○ A. huge   ○ B. hairless   ◉ C. amazing

4. From this paragraph, you can conclude that hippos
   ○ A. like to hide.   ◉ B. have sensitive skin.
   ○ C. are lazy.   ○ D. are night creatures.

1. Main Idea   2. Details   3. Point of View   4. Draw Conclusions

Name Rohan   **Date** 6/5/23

Read the paragraph. Then answer the questions.

Olympic Jobs

Everyone knows that thousands of athletes compete in the Olympic Games and that hundreds of thousands of visitors attend. But did you know that about 60,000 more people work to make the Olympics run smoothly? That's pretty impressive! Some of these workers are paid, but thousands of others are **volunteers**. All of them have to be trained for their job. These workers do everything from sweeping up litter to escorting competitors to selling tickets to announcing winners.

1. A title that best summarizes this paragraph is
   - ○ A. How Athletes Compete at the Games.
   - ○ B. Tips for Visitors to the Olympics.
   - ○ C. Working as a Ticket Seller.
   - ◉ D. Workers Behind the Olympics.

2. In this paragraph, the word **volunteers** means
   - ○ A. litter sweepers.   ◉ B. unpaid workers.
   - ○ C. competitors.   ○ D. athletic winners.

3. From this paragraph, you can conclude that
   - ○ A. the Olympics are a lot of fun.
   - ○ B. Olympic workers are paid well.
   - ◉ C. running the Olympics is a big job.
   - ○ D. most Olympic visitors help out.

4. Reread the paragraph. Write a sentence that is an opinion from the paragraph.

   "That's pretty impressive!"

   _____

Comprehension Skills: 40 Short Passages for Close Reading, Grade 4 © 2012 by Linda Ward Beech, Scholastic Teaching Resources

Name _Rohan_ Date _6 / 20 / 23_

Read the paragraph. Then answer the questions.

A Look at Leopards

Leopards hunt for their food at night. These animals are carnivores and eat only meat. Their excellent eyesight helps them stalk and capture their prey even in the dark. In many cases, a leopard will carry its prey long distances away from the place of the kill. Because it is a good climber, a leopard will often drag its dinner into a tree where other animals cannot reach it. There, the leopard can devour its meal alone. Unlike lions, leopards are solitary and **antisocial** animals.

1. In this paragraph, the word **antisocial** must mean
   - ○ A. friendly and likable.
   - ○ B. extremely hungry.
   - ○ C. enjoying groups.
   - ◉ D. not sociable.

2. The main idea of this paragraph is
   - ○ A. how leopards differ from lions.
   - ○ B. what leopards do during the day.
   - ○ C. what leopards eat for dinner.
   - ◉ D. how leopards hunt and eat.

3. Fill in the correct circle to show whether each statement is a fact or an inference.

   Fact Inference
   - ◉ ○ A. Leopards do not eat plants.
   - ◉ ○ B. Leopards can see very well.
   - ○ ◉ C. Leopard don't share their food.
   - ◉ ○ D. Leopards are good climbers.

4. Which phrase best reflects the writer's point of view?
   - ◉ A. respectful of leopards
   - ○ B. fearful of leopards
   - ○ C. amused by leopards

1. Context Clues 2. Main Idea 3. Inference 4. Point of View

Comprehension Skills: 40 Short Passages for Close Reading, Grade 4 © 2012 by Linda Ward Beech, Scholastic Teaching Resources

Name Rohan   **Date** 6/20/23

Read the paragraph. Then answer the questions.

Lunar New Year

The Lunar New Year lasts for 15 days and is observed by communities the world over. During this time, many special traditions are followed. One is the popular Dragon Dance, when people in a dragon costume twist and **prance** through the streets. On the last day of the New Year Celebration, when the full moon rises, people celebrate the Lantern Festival. Thousands of <u>paper and silk lanterns twinkle in the dark like magic stars</u>. This happy night embraces the New Year.

1. The underlined words in this paragraph are an example of figurative language called
- ○ A. metaphor.
- ○ B. personification.
- ◉ C. simile.
- ○ D. hyperbole.

2. Find and write another example of figurative language in the paragraph.

Personification

3. Which word in the paragraph is a clue to how the writer feels about Lunar New Year?
- ○ A. last
- ◉ B. special
- ○ C. full

4. In this paragraph, the word **prance** means
- ○ A. practice hard.
- ◉ B. dance playfully.
- ○ C. play tricks.
- ○ D. walk carefully.

Comprehension Skills: 40 Short Passages for Close Reading, Grade 4 © 2012 by Linda Ward Beech, Scholastic Teaching Resources

Name _Rohan_   **Date** _6/21/23_

Read the paragraph. Then answer the questions.

Pets in Paris

France has long been known as a country where people are devoted to their dogs. At some Paris hotels, this is no exception. They offer many services just for the canine set. For example, there are trained dog groomers, charming dog toiletries, and even custom-made beds for **pampered** pets. These hotels also provide round-the-clock room service for dogs, with a choice of healthy meals. Of course, dogs are welcome in the hotel restaurants, too. They can't get in without their owners, though!

1. Which phrase best reflects the writer's point of view?
   - ● A. approving of the dog treatment
   - ○ B. upset with the hotels
   - ○ C. outraged about so much attention being given to dogs

2. Write *fact* or *opinion* next to each sentence.
   - _fact_ A. They offer many services just for the canine set.
   - _fact_ B. These hotels also provide round-the-clock service for dogs.
   - _fact_ C. For example, there are charming dog toiletries.

3. From this paragraph, you can conclude that
   - ○ A. only Paris hotels have dog services.
   - ● B. dog services are big business in Paris.
   - ○ C. people aren't important to Paris hotels.
   - ○ D. cats are unpopular in Paris.

4. In this paragraph, the word **pampered** means
   - ○ A. wearing diapers.
   - ○ B. travel weary.
   - ● C. coddled.
   - ○ D. difficult.

Name _Rohan_   Date _6/21/23_

Read the paragraph. Then answer the questions.

Wigs and Gowns

In Britain, judges and lawyers have traditionally worn wigs and gowns in court. Depending on their role, some also wear lace neck trimmings, sashes, hoods, fur mantles, and buckled shoes. From time to time, this judicial finery has been mocked. After all, it is ridiculous. The curly wigs are made in four shades of off-white, ranging from light gray to beige. The more important the official, the fancier the wig. A senior judge wears a headpiece of curls that reaches to the shoulders. What a silly, fusty, dusty custom!

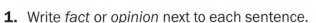

1. Write *fact* or *opinion* next to each sentence.

   fact A. In Britain, judges and lawyers have traditionally worn wigs and gowns in court.

   fact B. From time to time, this judicial finery has been mocked.

   opinion C. What a silly, fusty, dusty custom!

2. Which word in the paragraph is a clue to how the writer feels about court dress in Britain?
   - ● A. ridiculous
   - ○ B. important
   - ○ C. beige

3. Which sentence is most likely true?
   - ● A. Tradition is important in British courts.
   - ○ B. Judges wear wigs because they're bald.
   - ○ C. The curly wigs often fall off in court.
   - ○ D. Officials don't want to wear fancy wigs.

4. A title that best summarizes this paragraph is
   - ○ A. Curly Headpieces in Britain.
   - ● B. Traditional Court Dress in Britain.
   - ○ C. Light Gray to Beige.
   - ○ D. Laughing at Judicial Finery.

1. Fact & Opinion   2. Point of View   3. Inference   4. Summarize

Comprehension Skills: 40 Short Passages for Close Reading, Grade 4 © 2012 by Linda Ward Beech, Scholastic Teaching Resources

Name Rohan   **Date** 6/21/23

Read the paragraph. Then answer the questions.

Freecycling

You've heard of recycling, but do you know about freecycling? When you freecycle, you give away things you no longer want or need. Freecyclers can also acquire things that someone else is getting rid of. Lists of things available for freecycling and lists of things wanted by freecyclers are posted on Web sites. People who sign up and find just what they want then arrange to pick up the items. Some popular items for freecyclers are bicycles, exercise equipment, furniture, and computer parts.

1. Fill in the correct circle to show whether each statement is a fact or an inference.

Fact	Inference	
○	●	A. Freecycling is handy if you are cleaning a garage.
●	○	B. You could furnish a room from freecycled things.
●	○	C. Computer parts are favorite recycled items.
○	●	D. It's easiest to freecycle with people who are nearby.

2. Write *yes* or *no* under each heading on the chart to show if the word describes freecycling.

Costly	Dishonest	Useful
no	no	yes

3. The main idea of this paragraph is

○ A. how to get free things.   ○ B. how to get a used computer.

● C. extending the life of different items.   ○ D. getting rid of exercise equipment.

4. Which phrase best reflects the writer's point of view?

○ A. unimpressed with freecycling

○ B. worried about freecycling

● C. accepting of freecycling

1. Inference 2. Inference 3. Main Idea 4. Point of View

Comprehension Skills: 40 Short Passages for Close Reading, Grade 4 © 2012 by Linda Ward Beech, Scholastic Teaching Resources

Name _____ Date _____

Read the paragraph. Then answer the questions.

Madame C. J. Walker

When she was young, Madame C. J. Walker's hair began falling out. She tried a lot of remedies, but she was getting as bald as an egg. So she invented her own mixture—and it worked. Soon after, she decided to start her own hair-care business. At first, she sold her products door-to-door. Then she began selling products by mail. Madame Walker set up factories and opened beauty **parlors** in many cities. She also started training schools for her workers. By the time of her death in 1919, 25,000 women worked for Madame Walker. She was the first Black female millionaire. Much of her wealth went to help others.

1. From this paragraph, you can conclude that

○ A. Madame C. J. Walker was a good businesswoman.

○ B. Madame Walker's products were very expensive.

○ C. no one used hair products before Madame Walker.

○ D. most hair products today are sold door-to-door.

2. In this paragraph, the word **parlors** means

○ A. places used for parties.   ○ B. rooms used for business.

○ C. kinds of factories.   ○ D. training schools.

3. Fill in the correct circle to show whether each statement is a fact or an inference.

Fact   Inference

○   ○   A. Madame C. J. Walker was clever.

○   ○   B. She used the mail to sell her products.

○   ○   C. Madame C. J. Walker became a millionaire.

○   ○   D. Madame C. J. Walker was very generous.

4. Reread the paragraph. Find and write a simile from the paragraph.

_____

_____

1. Draw Conclusions   2. Context Clues   3. Inference   4. Figurative Language

Comprehension Skills: 40 Short Passages for Close Reading, Grade 4 © 2012 by Linda Ward Beech, Scholastic Teaching Resources

Name Rohan

Date 6/21/23

Read the paragraph. Then answer the questions.

From Gaggle to Gang

What is a gaggle? You probably know that it is a group of geese. *Gaggle* is a collective noun because it names a group. Many collective nouns _____ groups of animals. Some of these nouns are pretty amusing. For example, a string of ponies is a group of ponies, and a troop is a group of kangaroos. What is a knot? If you're talking about toads, then a knot is a group of them. Have you ever found foxes together? Then you saw a skulk. And if a group of elk crosses in front of you, you're looking at a gang.

1. The main idea of this paragraph is
   - ○ A. meanings of collective nouns.
   - ○ B. a knot is a group of toads.
   - ○ C. different kinds of groups.
   - ◉ D. how to use collective nouns.

2. A supporting detail is
   - ○ A. ants live in a colony.
   - ○ B. a gang is a group of elk.
   - ○ C. words with two meanings
   - ◉ D. singular and plural nouns

3. The best word for the blank in this paragraph is
   - ○ A. suggest.   ◉ B. define.
   - ○ C. question.   ○ D. answer.

4. Reread the paragraph. Find and write a sentence that is an opinion.

   "Have you ever found foxes together?"

1. Main Idea   2. Details   3. Context Clues   4. Fact & Opinion

Name _____ **Date** _____

Read the paragraph. Then answer the questions.

Spinning Spiders

You know that spiders spin silk, but do you know what spiders do with their silk? Mother spiders keep the eggs they lay in silk sacs. Spiders also use their silk to make webs or homes. Many spiders have hideouts in places such as window corners or under sills. They **line** the entrances to these places with silk. Spiders also use silk threads to drop straight to the ground when enemies appear. And clever spiders spin beautiful traps and nets to catch their dinner.

1. The title that best summarizes this paragraph is
   ○ A. How Spiders Find Food.
   ○ B. Spinning Silken Clothes.
   ○ C. A Spider's Use of Silk.
   ○ D. Outwitting Spider Enemies.

2. Write *fact* or *opinion* next to each sentence.
   _____ A. Spiders also use their silk to make webs or homes.
   _____ B. And clever spiders spin beautiful traps and nets to catch their dinner.
   _____ C. They line the entrances to these places with silk.

3. From this paragraph, you can conclude that
   ○ A. spiders like to eat their silk.
   ○ B. spiders use their silk for survival.
   ○ C. spider enemies try to steal the silk.
   ○ D. spider silk is weak and flimsy.

4. In this paragraph, the word **line** means
   ○ A. connect.   ○ B. persuade.
   ○ C. win over.   ○ D. cover.

Comprehension Skills: 40 Short Passages for Close Reading, Grade 4 © 2012 by Linda Ward Beech, Scholastic Teaching Resources

Name _____ Date_____

Read the paragraph. Then answer the questions.

Meet the Sloth

The sloth is a fascinating animal that lives in the trees of tropical forests in Central America. It spends much of its time hanging upside down from branches. A sloth moves very slowly, feeding on leaves and fruit as it goes. During the rainy season, a sloth has a greenish _____. Tiny plants called green algae live in the sloth's fur where they capture moisture from the rain. The algae provide **camouflage** for the sloth in the green treetops. Being able to blend in is very helpful because a sloth could never move quickly enough to escape its enemies.

1. The best word for the blank in this paragraph is
- ○ A. experience.
- ○ B. tinge.
- ○ C. offspring.
- ○ D. nutrition.

2. In this paragraph, the word **camouflage** must mean
- ○ A. concealment.
- ○ B. transportation.
- ○ C. flesh-eating.
- ○ D. entertainment.

3. The main idea of this paragraph is
- ○ A. what a sloth is like.
- ○ B. how camouflage helps a sloth.
- ○ C. where you can find a sloth.
- ○ D. sloths and the rainy season.

4. Which word in the paragraph is a clue to how the writer feels about sloths?
- ○ A. greenish
- ○ B. tropical
- ○ C. fascinating

Name _____ **Date** _____

Read the paragraph. Then answer the questions.

Learning About Tornados

Standing in front of a tornado is as risky as jumping off a cliff. But scientists have been trying to do something like this so they can find out how these storms work. In 1981, researchers designed a container called TOTO (Totable Tornado Observatory). Inside TOTO were hundreds of pounds of weather equipment. The idea was to place TOTO in the path of a tornado so its equipment could pick up information. However, scientists decided the experiment was as unsafe as a leaky boat and dropped the project.

1. The underlined words in this paragraph are an example of figurative language called
   - ○ A. metaphor.
   - ○ B. personification.
   - ○ C. simile.
   - ○ D. hyperbole.

2. Write *yes* or *no* under each heading on the chart to show if the word describes tornados.

Dangerous	Polluted	Pleasant

3. From this paragraph, you can conclude that
   - ○ A. scientists will try to use TOTO again.
   - ○ B. it's easy to study tornados.
   - ○ C. tornados pose challenges for scientists.
   - ○ D. it's fun to stand in front of tornados.

4. Reread the paragraph. Write a second figure of speech from the paragraph.

_____

_____

Name _____ **Date** _____

Read the paragraph. Then answer the questions.

Tale From the Deep

Scientists say that nature is really amazing. Recently, some scientists were studying a strange sponge found deep in the Pacific Ocean. They insisted that filaments on the sponge were much like optical fibers used in telecommunication systems. Their somewhat dubious plan was to study the sponge with the hope of **duplicating** its features for future uses. What those uses are, the scientists haven't said. Stay tuned!

1. Which word in the passage is a clue to how the writer feels about the scientists' plan of study?
   - ○ A. dubious
   - ○ B. amazing
   - ○ C. hope

2. In this paragraph, the word **duplicating** means
   - ○ A. changing.
   - ○ B. copying.
   - ○ C. studying.
   - ○ D. catching.

3. Which phrase best reflects the writer's point of view?
   - ○ A. awed by scientists and nature
   - ○ B. skeptical about the sponge study
   - ○ C. excited about the sponge project

4. The title that best summarizes this paragraph is
   - ○ A. Scientists Study Sponge.
   - ○ B. From the Pacific Ocean.
   - ○ C. A Sponge in Your Future.
   - ○ D. Filaments and Fibers.

1. Point of View   2. Context Clues   3. Point of View   4. Summarize

Name _____ Date_____

Read the paragraph. Then answer the questions.

Comic Strip Letters

Have you ever noticed that the print in comic strips is in capital letters? I find this really annoying. One reason given is that comic strips are reduced when printed in newspapers. When print is reduced, small letters tend to blob up more than big ones. Another reason is that by using letters that are the same height, an artist can fit them in the space more easily. I think that artists probably find using lowercase letters too much of a challenge. Maybe they don't know which words to capitalize!

CAPITALS FOR COMICS

1. Write *fact* or *opinion* next to each sentence.

   _____ A. Have you ever noticed that the print in comic strips is in capital letters?

   _____ B. When print is reduced, small letters tend to blob up more than big ones.

   _____ C. Maybe they don't know which words to capitalize!

2. The main idea of the paragraph is
   - A. the problems with small letters.
   - B. how artists use lowercase letters.
   - C. why capitalizing is important.
   - D. why capital letters are used in comics.

3. Which phrase best reflects the writer's point of view?
   - A. enthusiastic about capital letters in comics
   - B. indifferent to capital letters in comics
   - C. disapproving of capital letters in comics

4. From this paragraph, you can conclude that in comic strips
   - A. lowercase letters are easier to read.
   - B. reduced print is easier to read.
   - C. capital letters are easier to read.
   - D. letters of different heights look best.

1. Fact & Opinion   2. Main Idea   3. Point of View   4. Draw Conclusions

Name _____ Date_____

Read the paragraph. Then answer the questions.

Rodents on the Prairie

Prairie dogs are not really dogs; they're rodents. However, like canines, prairie dogs communicate by barking. Many of the sounds they make **alert** their colony to danger. For example, prairie dogs have one call for coyotes and another for hawks. When a coyote is sighted, other prairie dogs pop up from their burrows to keep track of where it goes. If a hawk is signaled, they dive into their burrows. Prairie dogs make still other sounds when humans are near. Most surprisingly, prairie dogs have distinct calls for different kinds of real dogs.

1. Fill in the correct circle to show whether each statement is a fact or an inference.

   Fact   Inference
   ○   ○   A. Prairie dogs are actually rodents.
   ○   ○   B. Hawks are bigger threats than coyotes.
   ○   ○   C. Prairie dogs make barking sounds.
   ○   ○   D. Prairie dogs have special calls for people.

2. The title that best summarizes this paragraph is
   ○ A. Watching for Coyotes.
   ○ B. How Prairie Dogs Communicate.
   ○ C. A Signal for Hawks.
   ○ D. Not Really Dogs.

3. In this paragraph, the word **alert** means
   ○ A. warn.   ○ B. ask.
   ○ C. bark.   ○ D. hide.

4. Which phrase best reflects the writer's point of view?
   ○ A. delighted by prairie dogs
   ○ B. interested in prairie dogs
   ○ C. bored by prairie dogs

1. Inference   2. Summarize   3. Context Clues   4. Point of View

Name _____ Date_____

Read the paragraph. Then answer the questions.

The Silk Route

Chinese people learned to make silk cloth almost 5,000 years ago. At that time, they were the only ones who knew how to make it. Soon traders from China found that people in the West would pay great prices for silk. So traders traveled long distances on camels across **harsh** deserts and over high mountains to sell their silk. They also brought styles of art and Chinese inventions, such as gunpowder, to the West. They returned with gold, nuts, perfumes, and goods from the West. This trade route became known as the Silk Route. It was awesome! Many of the stopping places on the route became great cities.

1. From this paragraph, you can conclude that
   - ○ A. travel on the Silk Route was safe and easy.
   - ○ B. gunpowder was an unimportant Chinese invention.
   - ○ C. ideas were also exchanged along the Silk Route.
   - ○ D. prices charged in the West for silk were too high.

2. Fill in the correct circle to show whether each statement is a fact or an inference.

   Fact   Inference
   - ○   ○   A. Long ago, silkmaking was a secret.
   - ○   ○   B. Traders made good money on the Silk Route.
   - ○   ○   C. Cities grew up along the Silk Route.
   - ○   ○   D. Traveling on the Silk Route was difficult.

3. Write *fact* or *opinion* next to each sentence.
   - _____ A. It was awesome!
   - _____ B. They returned with gold, nuts, perfumes, and goods from the West.
   - _____ C. Many of the stopping places on the route became great cities.

4. In this paragraph, the word **harsh** means
   - ○ A. large.   ○ B. comfortable.
   - ○ C. severe.   ○ D. pleasant.

1. Draw Conclusions   2. Inference   3. Fact & Opinion   4. Context Clues

Name _____ Date _____

Read the paragraph. Then answer the questions.

Happy Birthday

You turn a year older, and friends sing a certain song to you. The story of "Happy Birthday" goes back to the 1890s. In 1893 a teacher named Patty Smith Hill and her sister Mildred published a book called *Song Stories for Kindergarten.* The first song in the book was a four-line verse called "Good Morning to All." Patty soon wrote new words to this ditty, and it became the popular "Happy Birthday" song still sung today. People sing it in many languages around the world.

1. The main idea of this paragraph is
- ○ A. celebrating birthdays.
- ○ B. the story of "Happy Birthday."
- ○ C. kindergarten songs.
- ○ D. a worldwide song.

2. A supporting detail is
- ○ A. Mildred Hill was a church organist.
- ○ B. kindergartners like to sing.
- ○ C. Patty Hill wrote the words.
- ○ D. people in Nepal sing the song.

3. From this paragraph, you can conclude that
- ○ A. the birthday song is long.
- ○ B. kindergarteners are good singers.
- ○ C. people celebrate by singing on birthdays.
- ○ D. Patty Smith Hill knew many languages.

4. The title that best summarizes this paragraph is
- ○ A. Songs for Kindergarten.
- ○ B. How the Birthday Song Originated.
- ○ C. The Songs of Patty Smith Hill.
- ○ D. An 1893 Songbook.

1. Main Idea   2. Details   3. Draw Conclusions   4. Summarize

Name _____ **Date** _____

Read the paragraph. Then answer the questions.

Talking About Turtles

Turtles have been around for more than 200 million years.
<u>Covered by their shells, turtles are walking houses.</u>
Scientists think they are the most ancient of all reptiles.
Turtles live in many places on land and in water.
Like all reptiles, they are cold-blooded. Turtles that live
where winters are cold usually hibernate. Turtles eat
insects, fish, and frogs. They also munch on plants,
including fruit and flowers. The largest turtle is the
leatherback, which can weigh more than 2,000 pounds!
That's one huge reptile!

1. The title that best summarizes this paragraph is
   - ○ A. Interesting Facts About Turtles.
   - ○ B. The Large Leatherback.
   - ○ C. Very Ancient Reptiles.
   - ○ D. Places Where Turtles Live.

2. Write *fact* or *opinion* next to each sentence.
   - _____ A. Turtles eat insects, fish, and frogs.
   - _____ B. Turtles live in many places on land and water.
   - _____ C. That's one huge reptile!

3. Which phrase best reflects the writer's point of view?
   - ○ A. mystified by turtles
   - ○ B. appreciative of turtles
   - ○ C. uncertain about turtles

4. The underlined words in this paragraph are an example of figurative language called
   - ○ A. metaphor.   ○ B. personification.
   - ○ C. simile.   ○ D. hyperbole.

Name _____ Date_____

Read the paragraph. Then answer the questions.

Blobs on the Beach

Many things make scientists curious. For example, from time to time, large white blobs wash up onto beaches around the world. What are they? The _____ of a huge octopus? A giant squid? A sea monster? No one has ever been sure. Then, in 2003 a jelly-like blob washed up on the coast of Chile. This time a team of scientists used new tests to examine **specimens** of the enormous blob. This time they had an answer. The blob was not the remains of a sea monster, but old blubber from a whale.

1. The best word for the blank in this paragraph is
   - ○ A. remains.
   - ○ C. species.
   - ○ B. expressions.
   - ○ D. skeletons.

2. In this paragraph, the word **specimens** must mean
   - ○ A. long claws.
   - ○ C. monsters.
   - ○ B. tails and fins.
   - ○ D. examples.

3. The main idea of this paragraph is
   - ○ A. blobs on the coast of Chile.
   - ○ B. old blubber from a whale.
   - ○ C. identifying blobs on beaches.
   - ○ D. sea monsters on the beaches.

4. Fill in the correct circle to show whether each statement is a fact or an inference.

Fact	Inference	
○	○	A. People are curious about blobs on beaches.
○	○	B. Blobs are deposited on beaches by tides.
○	○	C. Scientists have studied samples from blobs.
○	○	D. So far, blobs have not come from sea monsters.

1. Context Clues   2. Context Clues   3. Main Idea   4. Inference

Name _____ Date_____

Read the paragraph. Then answer the questions.

Meriwether Lewis

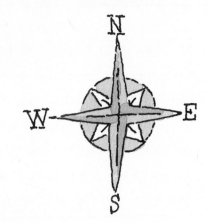

In 1802, Meriwether Lewis began preparations to explore the land from the Mississippi River to the Rocky Mountains. <u>You would have thought that Lewis was going to the moon</u>. He studied maps. He learned how to take measurements by the stars to figure out directions. He ordered guns and supplies. He talked to geographers, botanists, and zoologists. He had a keelboat built. He chose a co-leader, William Clark, and a crew. Adventure called, and in 1804 the team set off.

1. The underlined words in this paragraph are an example of figurative language called
   - ○ A. metaphor.
   - ○ B. personification.
   - ○ C. simile.
   - ○ D. hyperbole.

2. Find and write another example of figurative language in the paragraph.

   _____

   _____

3. The main idea of this paragraph is
   - ○ A. ordering guns and supplies.
   - ○ B. choosing a co-leader to lead the team.
   - ○ C. how Lewis prepared to explore.
   - ○ D. going to the moon.

4. Reread the paragraph. What inference can you make about Meriwether Lewis?

   _____

   _____

Name _____ **Date** _____

Read the paragraph. Then answer the questions.

Wake-Up Call

I was awakened from a deep sleep the other morning by the awful noise of a car alarm. It was the kind that goes off in an unpleasant, repetitive way every few minutes. Finally, someone came and drove the offending vehicle away. The next morning, I awoke to the same **annoying** sound. When I looked out the window, there was no car. All I saw was a mockingbird on my fence. And sure enough, that remarkable bird was imitating a car alarm. I have to admit it was quite a performance.

1. What is the writer's point of view about car alarms?

_____

_____

2. Which word in the passage is a clue to what the writer thinks of the mockingbird?
- ○ A. offending
- ○ B. repetitive
- ○ C. remarkable

3. In this paragraph, the word **annoying** means
- ○ A. loud.
- ○ B. repetitive.
- ○ C. bothersome.
- ○ D. soothing.

4. Write *fact* or *opinion* next to each sentence.

_____ A. All I saw was a mockingbird on my fence.

_____ B. When I looked out the window, there was no car.

_____ C. I have to admit it was quite a performance.

Name _____ Date_____

Read the paragraph. Then answer the questions.

Snowflakes

How lucky we are when snow begins to fall! Something beautiful is coming our way because the geometry of a snowflake is spectacular. Snowflakes form when water vapor condenses into crystals. Although snowflakes are never identical, they all have a six-pointed symmetry in common. However, weather conditions affect the final shape of a snowflake. These conditions include the temperature and the amount of water vapor in the air. Each snowflake is a work of art.

1. Write *fact* or *opinion* next to each sentence.

    _____ A. How lucky we are when snow begins to fall!

    _____ B. Something beautiful is coming our way because the geometry of a snowflake is spectacular.

    _____ C. Although snowflakes are never identical, they all have a six-pointed symmetry in common.

2. The underlined words in this paragraph are an example of figurative language called

    ○ A. metaphor.   ○ B. personification.

    ○ C. simile.   ○ D. hyperbole.

3. Which phrase best reflects the writer's point of view?

    ○ A. suspicious of snowflakes

    ○ B. admiring of snowflakes

    ○ C. shocked by snowflakes

4. The title that best summarizes this paragraph is

    ○ A. How Snowflakes Form.

    ○ B. Vapor Into Crystals.

    ○ C. Six-Pointed Shapes.

    ○ D. Something Beautiful.

Name _____ Date _____

Read the paragraph. Then answer the questions.

Watch the Weather

The organizers of the Olympics face many problems. One of the biggest is often the weather. In the years 1932, 1956, and 1964, a lack of snow made things difficult at the Winter Olympics. Scorching temperatures during some Summer Olympics have also caused problems. In 1924, only half of the runners in a cross-country event made it to the finish line because of the heat. <u>Other weather-related problems have created headaches, too</u>. In 1896 in Greece, the rowing races had to be cancelled because the sea was too rough. A flood once almost halted the Olympics in Paris.

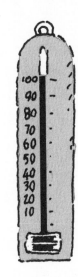

1. Fill in the correct circle to show whether each statement is a fact or an inference.

Fact   Inference

◯   ◯   A. A lack of snow has threatened the Winter Olympics.

◯   ◯   B. Weather conditions affect the Olympic Games.

◯   ◯   C. Olympic organizers have to be good problem solvers.

◯   ◯   D. High temperatures can be a problem in the Summer Games.

2. The main idea of this paragraph is
   ◯ A. rough seas at the Olympics.
   ◯ B. Winter Olympics' lack of snow.
   ◯ C. too much heat at the Olympics
   ◯ D. weather problems at the Olympics.

3. The underlined words in this paragraph are an example of figurative language called
   ◯ A. metaphor.   ◯ B. personification.
   ◯ C. simile.   ◯ D. hyperbole.

4. Which phrase best reflects the writer's point of view?
   ◯ A. impatient with weather problems
   ◯ B. understanding of weather problems
   ◯ C. outraged about weather problems

1. Inference   2. Main Idea   3. Figurative Language   4. Point of View

Comprehension Skills: 40 Short Passages for Close Reading, Grade 4 © 2012 by Linda Ward Beech, Scholastic Teaching Resources

Name _____ Date_____

Read the paragraph. Then answer the questions.

Chippy the Chimp

The phone at a zoo in Scotland kept ringing, but no one spoke when the employees answered. The only sound was a kind of snuffling noise. This went on for two nights. Everyone was mystified. Then an employee found the **prankster**. It was Chippy, an 11-year-old chimp who had snatched a cell phone from one of his keepers. To make his calls, Chippy had been hitting the "redial" button. Thanks to Chippy's cellular monkey business, the zookeeper's phone bill was rather high that month! Since then, the keeper stores his cell phone in a deep pocket.

1. From this paragraph, you can conclude that
   - ○ A. Chippy was playing with the cell phone.
   - ○ B. Chippy wanted to scare the zoo employees.
   - ○ C. Chippy had to pay for all the calls he made.
   - ○ D. Chippy knew the telephone number of the zoo.

2. In this paragraph, the word **prankster** means
   - ○ A. problem.   ○ B. trickster.
   - ○ C. zookeeper.   ○ D. criminal.

3. Which phrase best reflects the writer's point of view?
   - ○ A. surprised by Chippy's behavior
   - ○ B. unhappy with Chippy's actions
   - ○ C. tickled by Chippy's story

4. The main idea of this paragraph is
   - ○ A. a careless zookeeper.
   - ○ B. a high phone bill.
   - ○ C. snuffling noises on the phone.
   - ○ D. a chimp's cell phone calls.

1. Draw Conclusions 2. Context Clues 3. Point of View 4. Main Idea

Comprehension Skills: 40 Short Passages for Close Reading, Grade 4 © 2012 by Linda Ward Beech, Scholastic Teaching Resources

Name _____ Date _____

Read the paragraph. Then answer the questions.

Finding Food

When the first English settlers arrived in America, they were amazed at the foods they found. The Native peoples had developed **techniques** for growing corn, squash, watermelons, and other crops. The settlers also found blueberries, cranberries, wild rice, and pumpkin. They learned to eat lobster and crab as well as cod and striped bass. Still other foods included nuts such as cashews, black walnuts, hickory nuts, and pecans. Wild turkeys were also a first for the settlers.

1. The main idea of this paragraph is
   - ○ A. local foods found by English settlers.
   - ○ B. a variety of new nuts to eat.
   - ○ C. how Native Americans caught seafood.
   - ○ D. berries were plentiful.

2. A supporting detail is
   - ○ A. a new menu for the settlers.
   - ○ B. kidney and lima beans were good.
   - ○ C. the settlers ate their first turkey.
   - ○ D. native foods were delicious.

3. In this paragraph, the word **techniques** means
   - ○ A. farming tools.   ○ B. ways of doing things.
   - ○ C. kinds of plants.   ○ D. special containers.

4. A title that best summarizes this paragraph is
   - ○ A. Blueberries and Cranberries.
   - ○ B. Food From the Sea.
   - ○ C. English Settlers in America.
   - ○ D. Plentiful Produce for Settlers.

Comprehension Skills: 40 Short Passages for Close Reading, Grade 4 © 2012 by Linda Ward Beech, Scholastic Teaching Resources

1. Main Idea 2. Details 3. Context Clues 4. Summarize

Name _____ Date _____

Read the paragraph. Then answer the questions.

Earthquakes and Buildings

Earthquakes cause buildings to fall and injure or kill people. So engineers and architects are trying to make buildings safer. It's about time! Skyscrapers are built so that they sway but don't fall when earthquakes **strike**. Some buildings are put on rollers while others have steel beams anchored into the ground. Builders also use stronger and more flexible materials. A new idea is to put heavy weights in buildings so that if they move one way, the weight moves the other way to help keep the building from toppling.

1. How do earthquakes harm people? _____

_____

2. Write *yes* or *no* under each heading on the chart to show if the word describes earthquake damage.

Harmful	Modern	Costly

3. Write *fact* or *opinion* next to each sentence.

_____ A. So engineers and architects are trying to make buildings safer.

_____ B. It's about time!

_____ C. Earthquakes cause buildings to fall and injure or kill people.

4. In this paragraph, the word **strike** means

○ A. swing. ○ B. fall.

○ C. hit. ○ D. kill.

Comprehension Skills: 40 Short Passages for Close Reading, Grade 4 © 2012 by Linda Ward Beech, Scholastic Teaching Resources

Name _____ Date_____

Read the paragraph. Then answer the questions.

Off-Duty and On-Duty

Kato is a dog that likes to get around. Kato lives at
an amusement park. Many of his hours are spent working
as a guard dog on the night _____. But when Kato
is off-duty, he likes to ride on the Ferris wheel. In fact,
Kato has his own customized car. The benches have been
removed so he has enough room, and bowls of food
and water are provided. Sometimes Kato rides for hours.
Other riders always ask about the Ferris wheel dog,
but they aren't allowed to ride in his **compartment**.

1. The best word for the blank in this paragraph is
    ○ A. time.   ○ B. shift.
    ○ C. canine.   ○ D. attack.

2. From this paragraph, you can conclude that
    ○ A. Kato is not a good worker.
    ○ B. Kato gets dizzy on the Ferris wheel.
    ○ C. Kato is greatly appreciated at the park.
    ○ D. Kato eats a lot while working.

3. In this paragraph, the word **compartment** must mean
    ○ A. a section.
    ○ B. workplace.
    ○ C. amusement park.
    ○ D. curiosity.

4. The main idea of this paragraph is
    ○ A. riding on the Ferris wheel.
    ○ B. a customized car for a dog.
    ○ C. working as a guard dog.
    ○ D. the life of an amusement park dog.

Comprehension Skills: 40 Short Passages for Close Reading, Grade 4 © 2012 by Linda Ward Beech, Scholastic Teaching Resources

1. Context Clues 2. Draw Conclusions 3. Context Clues 4. Main Idea

Name _____ Date_____

Read the paragraph. Then answer the questions.

Shoe Story

<u>A shoe by the roadside is an untold story</u>. Where is the mate? How did it get there? Many people are curious about shoes lying on the sides of roads. They have come up with several explanations. One idea is that the shoes were tossed out of cars by children during arguments. Another idea is that hikers accidentally dropped a shoe. A third **theory** is that the shoes fell out of garbage trucks. No one knows for sure. These single roadside shoes don't tell their secret.

1. The underlined words in this paragraph are an example of figurative language called
   - ○ A. metaphor.
   - ○ B. personification.
   - ○ C. simile.
   - ○ D. hyperbole.

2. A title that best summarizes this paragraph is
   - ○ A. Missing Mate.
   - ○ B. Off of Trucks.
   - ○ C. Roadside Shoes.
   - ○ D. Litter or Not?

3. In this paragraph, the word **theory** means
   - ○ A. therapy.
   - ○ B. secret.
   - ○ C. story.
   - ○ D. explanation.

4. Reread the paragraph. Find and write another example of figurative language.

   _____

   _____

Comprehension Skills: 40 Short Passages for Close Reading, Grade 4 © 2012 by Linda Ward Beech, Scholastic Teaching Resources

Name _____ Date_____

Read the paragraph. Then answer the questions.

Festival of Lights

Diwali is a happy and delightful holiday that is celebrated by Hindus around the world. Diwali is sometimes called the Festival of Lights. Lamps brighten streets, line building rooftops, and shine from windows. Hindus believe that Lakshmi, the goddess of wealth, uses the lamps to guide her way as she comes to bless homes. Diwali also symbolizes the victory of good over evil. For Hindus, this holiday is the beginning of the New Year. People wear new clothes and eat special foods on this very festive day.

1. Which phrase best reflects the writer's point of view?
   - ○ A. fearful about this holiday
   - ○ B. enthusiastic about this holiday
   - ○ C. indifferent to this holiday

2. Write *fact* or *opinion* next to each sentence.
   _____ A. Lamps brighten streets, line building rooftops, and shine from windows.
   _____ B. Diwali is sometimes called the Festival of Lights.
   _____ C. Diwali is a happy and delightful holiday that is celebrated by Hindus around the world.

3. The title that best summarizes this paragraph is
   - ○ A. Good Over Evil.   ○ B. The New Year.
   - ○ C. Understanding Diwali.   ○ D. Lots of Lights.

4. Fill in the correct circle to show whether each statement is a fact or an inference.

Fact	Inference	
○	○	A. People look forward to Diwali.
○	○	B. Lakshmi is the goddess of wealth.
○	○	C. Diwali is important to Hindus.
○	○	D. People shop to prepare for Diwali.

1. Point of View 2. Fact & Opinion 3. Summarize 4. Inference

Name _____ Date_____

Read the paragraph. Then answer the questions.

Civil War Game

A good way to spend free time is by playing games. During the Civil War (1861–1865), both Union and Confederate soldiers had time between battles. So the troops amused themselves in different ways. The Union soldiers played a popular board game called "The Checkered Game of Life." It was such a terrific game! Whoever invented it must have been very clever. A **version** of this game is still around today. It is now called "The Game of Life." Have you ever played it?

1. Write *fact* or *opinion* next to each sentence.

   _____ A. The Union soldiers played a popular board game called "The Checkered Game of Life."

   _____ B. A good way to spend free time is by playing games.

   _____ C. It was such a terrific game!

2. In this paragraph, the word **version** means
   ○ A. verse.   ○ B. revival.
   ○ C. form.   ○ D. battle.

3. Which phrase best reflects the writer's point of view?
   ○ A. supportive of a Civil War game
   ○ B. distressed by a Civil War game
   ○ C. disappointed by a Civil War game

4. Reread the paragraph. Find and write another opinion.

   _____

   _____

1. Fact & Opinion   2. Context Clues   3. Point of View   4. Fact & Opinion

Comprehension Skills: 40 Short Passages for Close Reading, Grade 4 © 2012 by Linda Ward Beech, Scholastic Teaching Resources

Name _____ Date_____

Read the paragraph. Then answer the questions.

Desert Cat

It's fast, strong, and a very good hunter. It can catch sand rats, jerboas, and ground squirrels. It is also known for its jumping skills, which it uses when hunting birds. What is this animal? It's the caracal, a cat that lives in the deserts of Africa, the Middle East, and parts of Asia. The caracal has short, sleek hair that is reddish-brown in color. Its large, pointed ears are black on the back. Usually, the caracal does its hunting at night to **avoid** the hot temperatures of the desert in daytime.

1. Fill in the correct circle to show whether each statement is a fact or an inference.

   Fact   Inference
   ○   ○   A. The caracal is a wild animal.
   ○   ○   B. Temperatures in the desert drop at night.
   ○   ○   C. The caracal can jump when catching birds.
   ○   ○   D. The caracal is a carnivore.

2. The main idea of this paragraph is
   ○ A. the jumping skills of the caracal.   ○ B. the homeland of the caracal.
   ○ C. the hunting skills of the caracal.   ○ D. the hunting prey of the caracal.

3. In this paragraph, the word **avoid** means
   ○ A. seek.   ○ B. alter.
   ○ C. evade.   ○ D. use.

4. From this paragraph, you can conclude that the caracal
   ○ A. likes being out at night.   ○ B. is a popular pet in Africa.
   ○ C. is well adapted for the desert. ○ D. often goes hungry.

Comprehension Skills: 40 Short Passages for Close Reading, Grade 4 © 2012 by Linda Ward Beech, Scholastic Teaching Resources

1. Inference   2. Main Idea   3. Context Clues   4. Draw Conclusions

Name _____ Date_____

Read the paragraph. Then answer the questions.

Fence of Colors

Passing motorists often think they have stumbled onto a huge art installation. Instead, they are going by a testing ground for a paint company. About 20,000 wood panels covered with paint and stain stand on a farm in New Jersey. The result is acres and acres of every shade of color. <u>It's a huge rainbow</u>. By leaving these panels out in each season and all kinds of weather, the company learns how well and how long the paint holds up. Still, as one house painter points out, "No matter how good the paint is, you have to prepare the surface well first."

1. From this paragraph, you can conclude that
   - ○ A. yellow is the company's biggest seller.
   - ○ B. the company is testing exterior paint.
   - ○ C. the company also tests competitors' paint.
   - ○ D. the paint panels are changed every month.

2. The underlined words in this paragraph are an example of figurative language called
   - ○ A. metaphor.
   - ○ B. personification.
   - ○ C. simile.
   - ○ D. hyperbole.

3. The title that best summarizes this paragraph is
   - ○ A. Paint in All Kinds of Weather.
   - ○ B. A Surprise for Passing Motorists.
   - ○ C. Acres and Acres of Color Panels.
   - ○ D. A Testing Ground for a Paint Company.

4. Which phrase best reflects the writer's point of view?
   - ○ A. intrigued by the wood panels
   - ○ B. disgusted about the wood panels
   - ○ C. bewildered by the wood panels

Comprehension Skills: 40 Short Passages for Close Reading, Grade 4 © 2012 by Linda Ward Beech, Scholastic Teaching Resources

Name _____ Date _____

Read the paragraph. Then answer the questions.

Presidential Nicknames

Many U.S. presidents have had nicknames. Calvin Coolidge was known as Silent Cal because he rarely spoke. The Little Magician was Martin Van Buren, who wore a tall silk hat. Grover Cleveland earned the nickname Veto President because he vetoed more bills than all **previous** presidents combined. Andrew Jackson's nickname was Old Hickory, while Theodore Roosevelt's was Rough Rider. The Great Emancipator was Abraham Lincoln, who wrote a proclamation that emancipated, or freed, people who were enslaved.

1. The main idea of this paragraph is
   - ○ A. Grover Cleveland vetoed many bills.
   - ○ B. many presidents have had nicknames.
   - ○ C. not all nicknames are flattering.
   - ○ D. everyone should have a nickname.

2. A supporting detail is
   - ○ A. nicknames are given fondly.
   - ○ B. Lincoln was the greatest president.
   - ○ C. Calvin Coolidge was talkative.
   - ○ D. Andrew Jackson was Old Hickory.

3. From this paragraph, you can conclude that
   - ○ A. not all nicknames are flattering.
   - ○ B. nicknames are only for Presidents.
   - ○ C. Presidents choose their own nicknames.
   - ○ D. nicknames show popularity.

4. In this paragraph, the word **previous** means
   - ○ A. older.
   - ○ B. later.
   - ○ C. precious.
   - ○ D. earlier.

1. Main Idea   2. Details   3. Draw Conclusions   4. Context Clues

Name _____ Date _____

Read the paragraph. Then answer the questions.

Buddy and Frank

Buddy was the first seeing-eye dog in the United States.
Despite the name, she was really a female. This German
shepherd was trained at a place called Fortunate Fields in
Switzerland in the 1920s. Then she was matched with
a blind American named Morris Frank. He and Buddy
learned to work together. When they returned to the
United States, Frank started a school to train more guide
dogs. It was called the Seeing Eye. Today, the school is in
Morristown, New Jersey. Each year, it **matches** 300 blind
people with dogs like Buddy.

1. Who was Buddy? _____

_____

2. Write *yes* or *no* under each heading on the chart to show if the word
describes seeing-eye dogs.

Playful	Helpful	Schooled

3. From this paragraph, you can conclude that seeing-eye dogs
- ○ A. all come from Switzerland.
- ○ B. are all German shepherds.
- ○ C. are important to the blind.
- ○ D. are all trained in New Jersey.

4. In this paragraph, the word **matches** means
- ○ A. lighters.
- ○ B. separates.
- ○ C. puts together.
- ○ D. trains.

1. Summarize   2. Inference   3. Draw Conclusions   4. Context Clues

Comprehension Skills: 40 Short Passages for Close Reading: Grade 4 • © 2012 by Linda Ward Beech, Scholastic Teaching Resources

Name _____ **Date** _____

Read the paragraph. Then answer the questions.

Choosing Leaders

People have been voting for their leaders since at least 500 B.C. Some of the earliest voters were ancient Greek citizens. They voted by dropping clay balls into pots for the _____ of their choice. Centuries later, Roman citizens voted with beans. Early settlers in North America used corn kernels. In the 1800s, people marked their choices on paper **ballots**. By 1892, voters were using machines with levers, and in the 1960s punch cards became common. Today, electronic voting is becoming widespread.

1. The best word for the blank in this paragraph is
   - ○ A. candidates.
   - ○ B. elections.
   - ○ C. stew.
   - ○ D. authentic.

2. The title that best summarizes this paragraph is
   - ○ A. Dropping Clay Balls.
   - ○ B. Voting Over Time.
   - ○ C. Why People Vote.
   - ○ D. Using Beans and Corn.

3. In this paragraph, the word **ballots** must mean
   - ○ A. songs sung by wandering groups.
   - ○ B. printed pages for registering votes.
   - ○ C. a kind of dance on toe shoes.
   - ○ D. pens used by people voting.

4. From this paragraph, you can conclude that
   - ○ A. voters will return to using machines with levers.
   - ○ B. how people vote will continue to change.
   - ○ C. paper ballots are the most popular way to vote.
   - ○ D. ways of voting will not improve.

1. Context Clues 2. Summarize 3. Context Clues 4. Draw Conclusions

Name _____ **Date**_____

Read the paragraph. Then answer the questions.

Tail Tales

<u>Animal tails tell many tales</u>. In most cases, an animal's tail serves a helpful function. For example, the tail of a bird helps it fly. A porcupine's tail is a weapon. The porcupine uses the many quills in its tail to defend itself. A horse uses its tail to keep away flies. Fish, of course, use their tails to help them swim. What does an elephant use its tail for? A baby elephant holds onto its mother's tail with its trunk so it doesn't get lost. Isn't that cute? Kangaroos use their tails for balance. They can also sit on their tails!

1. The underlined words in this paragraph are an example of figurative language called
   - ○ A. metaphor.
   - ○ B. personification.
   - ○ C. simile.
   - ○ D. hyperbole.

2. Write *fact* or *opinion* next to each sentence.
   - _____ A. A porcupine's tail is a weapon.
   - _____ B. Isn't that cute?
   - _____ C. A horse uses its tail to keep away flies.

3. The title that best summarizes this paragraph is
   - ○ A. Kangaroos Use Tails for Balance.
   - ○ B. Tails Help Birds Fly.
   - ○ C. Some Tails Have Quills.
   - ○ D. How Tails Help Animals.

4. Fill in the correct circle to show whether each statement is a fact or an inference.

   Fact Inference
   - ○   ○   A. A horse uses its tail to swat flies.
   - ○   ○   B. Tails can help protect an animal.
   - ○   ○   C. A baby elephant holds its mother tail.
   - ○   ○   D. Tails can help keep an animal comfortable.

1. Figurative Language 2. Fact & Opinion 3. Summarize 4. Inference

Name _____ Date _____

Read the paragraph. Then answer the questions.

Stop and Go

Streets were a mess in 1923. Not only that, they were downright dangerous. Cars drove through intersections without stopping. So did horse-drawn carriages and bicyclists. Lots of accidents happened, and many people were injured. Then Garrett Morgan invented the electric traffic signal. What a difference! Now drivers knew when to proceed or stop. Morgan's ingenious invention, one of many he made in his lifetime, was the beginning of the traffic light system we use today. This inventor should be thanked!

1. Which word in the passage is a clue to how the writer feels about this invention?
   - ○ A. dangerous
   - ○ B. electric
   - ○ C. ingenious

2. Write *fact* or *opinion* next to each sentence.
   - _____ A. This inventor should be thanked!
   - _____ B. Cars drove through intersections without stopping.
   - _____ C. What a difference!

3. The main idea of this paragraph is
   - ○ A. traffic problems in 1923.
   - ○ B. collisions of horse-drawn carriages and bicyclists.
   - ○ C. how the electric traffic signal improved traffic.
   - ○ D. the inventions of Garrett Morgan.

4. From this paragraph, you can conclude that
   - ○ A. accidents increased after the traffic signal was invented.
   - ○ B. Garrett Morgan made a lot of money on his invention.
   - ○ C. horses learned how to read electric traffic signals.
   - ○ D. accidents decreased after the traffic signal was invented.

Name _____ Date _____

Read the paragraph. Then answer the questions.

Mighty Mountains

A huge mountain system **stretches** across 1,500 miles of Asia. This mountain range is called the Himalayas. The mountains were formed about 60 million years ago. The world's 10 tallest mountains are all in the Himalayas. That's amazing! Mount Everest, which lies between Tibet and Nepal, is the world's highest mountain. It reaches up 29,028 feet in the air, too high for even birds to fly. The first climbers to reach the top did so in 1953. They must have been brave. Their names were Sir Edmund Hillary and Tenzing Norgay.

1. Write *fact* or *opinion* next to each sentence.

   _____ A. This mountain range is called the Himalayas.

   _____ B. They must have been brave.

   _____ C. The world's 10 tallest mountains are all in the Himalayas.

2. In this paragraph, the word **stretches** means
   - A. yawns.
   - B. extends.
   - C. climbs.
   - D. forms.

3. From this paragraph, you can conclude that all mountain ranges are
   - A. called the Himalayas.
   - B. made up of many mountains.
   - C. only in Asia.
   - D. were formed about 60 million years ago.

4. Reread the paragraph. Find and write another opinion.

   _____

   _____

Name _____ **Date**_____

Read the paragraph. Then answer the questions.

Word Pairs

Have you ever **noticed** how some words are used together all the time? <u>It's as if they were partners</u>. For example, people often say "mix and match" or "nuts and bolts." Other words that are often paired are "kiss and tell," "wash and dry," and "meat and potatoes." Perhaps you have used a few of these phrases, too. How many times have you said you were "sick and tired" of something? Have you ever ordered food that was "sweet and sour"? And no doubt you've spent time most days putting on your "socks and shoes."

1. Fill in the correct circle to show whether each statement is a fact or an inference.

Fact   Inference
○   ○   A. An example of paired words is "meat and potatoes."
○   ○   B. People get in the habit of using certain words together.
○   ○   C. The words "socks and shoes" are often used together.
○   ○   D. Words used together have a catchy sound.

2. The underlined words in this paragraph are an example of figurative language called
○ A. metaphor.   ○ B. personification.
○ C. simile.   ○ D. hyperbole.

3. In this paragraph, the word **noticed** means
○ A. heard.   ○ B. wondered.
○ C. observed.   ○ D. asked.

4. The main idea of this paragraph is
○ A. people often say "mix and match."
○ B. some words don't go together well.
○ C. why people say "meat and potatoes."
○ D. words that are often said together.

Name _____   Date _____

Read the paragraph. Then answer the questions.

Short Forms

When a word has been shortened, it is called a clip.
For example, a *ref* is a short form of the word *referee*.
Over time, many words in English have been **clipped**.
Do you know the original word for a *mike*? It's *microphone*.
Something that is a *curio* was once a *curiosity*. You probably
enjoy visiting the *zoo*, but at one time people visited
a *zoological garden*. Perhaps you go to and from school
on a *bus*. Students of the past traveled on an *omnibus*.
School words such as *math* and *exams* are simplified
versions of *mathematics* and *examinations*.

1. From this paragraph, you can conclude that
- ○ A. it is harder to learn clipped words.
- ○ B. riding on an omnibus was not safe.
- ○ C. clips are easier to pronounce and spell.
- ○ D. people don't like to use short words.

2. Which phrase best reflects the writer's point of view?
- ○ A. disbelieving
- ○ B. upset
- ○ C. neutral

3. The main idea of this paragraph is
- ○ A. from *mathematics* to *math*.
- ○ B. words that have been shortened over time.
- ○ C. *zoological garden* or *zoo*?
- ○ D. why words have been clipped.

4. In this paragraph, the word **clipped** means
- ○ A. changed.   ○ B. stolen.
- ○ C. hit.   ○ D. shortened.